stumbling stones

a path through grief, love and loss

airdre grant

hardie grant books

Published in 2016 by Hardie Grant Books

Hardie Grant Books (Australia)
Ground Floor, Building 1
658 Church Street
Richmond, Victoria 3121
www.hardiegrant.com.au

Hardie Grant Books (UK)
5th & 6th Floors
52–54 Southwark Street
London SE1 1UN
www.hardiegrant.co.uk

'High Country Weather' reproduced with permission from the James K Baxter estate.

Cataloguing-in-Publication data is available from the catalogue of the
National Library of Australia at www.nla.gov.au.

Stumbling Stones
ISBN 978 1 74379 057 1

Typesetting by Kirby Jones
Cover design by Rihana Ries
Illustrations by Niki Paronak/Shutterstock
Printed in China by 1010 Printing International Limited

To Angus, of course

Contents

The descent

It was a sunny Sunday afternoon when the phone rang. I was idly wondering if I had the will to vacuum. The siren call of the phone offered a reprieve. It was my big brother calling to tell me that my twin brother, Angus, was dead. That's all he said, 'He's dead.'

I fell spinning into an abyss of pain and darkness. I shook and I wept. Food repelled me. I couldn't sit still let alone drive. Sleep was ragged. My skin felt paper thin and my sensitivity was acute. The pain was unremitting. CS Lewis said in *A Grief Observed* that the death of a beloved is an amputation. For a twin it's worse. I couldn't move. My dog came and sat next to me.

Alone in his flat, Angus died when an ulcer had burst.

It wasn't my first encounter with the sharp pain of grief and loss, but I forgot it and had been living with the blithe arrogance of everyday life. My concerns up until that moment were parking, work, bills. I didn't think about pain. Brutalities and wars in faraway countries didn't really affect me. I had forgotten how grief walks alongside, sits on your shoulders. At any time your proud little house of cards can tumble down.

Years ago I had confidently asserted that pain was an ally. I didn't remember how it strips you back to your core, naked for all to see, defenceless, wounded and raw. Time tricked me into thinking I had learned the strong, driving nature of this lesson. I realise now this was foolishness.

I did remember how people behaved toward the bereaved, though. Their awkwardness and muffled kindness. The way they changed around me. Some ran a million miles, as if I were carrying a terrifying infection. Others drew close. Too close. Treating me as if I were ill, they patted my arm, looked deeply into my eyes and whispered in voices dripping with concern, 'Are you okay?' No, I'm not, I would think, pulling away. Please don't make my pain your story. Leave me alone. It was hard to receive kindness and even harder from friends than from strangers.

I was given curious gifts in that ragged time: sure knowledge of what I would and wouldn't do, crystal-clear knowing of what really mattered. The trivialities of life were exposed baldly. People's vanities shone brightly. I was released from worrying about what others thought of me.

The whole business of grief and loss is a mess. It can start badly and end who knows how or when. It doesn't have to be about death. It can be about loss of a friendship, a pet, a dream of you, vitality, country, hair, strength. It's not always as straightforward as death, where the loss is there for all to see. What about those mysterious unresolved losses? Babies adopted out in secrecy, the end of a forbidden relationship?

Whatever way you come to it, the journey through grief is long and unpredictable. The only way through it is through it. There are no shortcuts. The more you step into it, the better. Avoidance only brings it back more strongly later on. Better to lash yourself to the mast and sail into the storm. What choice do you have? And after others have tired of you and gone back to their lives, you still have to sail that sea. Things happen on that journey. Friendships are formed and gifts arrive from unexpected sources. A friend told me once, 'You get the help you need, not when you think you need it, but when you really need it.' She was right.

Dear God, I miss my twin. It's called being twinless and I am told there are support groups, even conferences. Only a twin understands how awful it is when your kindred spirit is gone. For the first time in my life I was really alone. And yet, I feel him around me; I know he watches over me.

Just as I was getting a wee bit better, my dog died. With sadness, I buried him in my garden.

Then my father died. Now the descent accelerated. It had started when I visited him at the nursing home and found him asleep on the chair. He started at my touch and said, 'Dear, it is good to see you.' It smote my heart.

With encouragement, I managed to get him into a wheelchair and out to the car. After some painful hefting and shoving we were off. I drove to a nearby park with level paths where I could wheel him to look at the ocean inlet, the sea glistening on the mudflats.

He was so frail. Paper skin, bony hands, cold feet in felt slippers; he sat in semi-regal splendour with his Russian hat and a warm blanket across scrawny knees. Once a powerful man, one that I feared, he was now fragile and diminished. A husk. Nearly deaf, nearly blind, with difficulty moving, he had suffered so much loss—dignity, privacy, vigour and influence. All were gone. He had been banned from taking alcohol, which he loved, so I plied him cheerfully with brandy and soda, and he sipped it, gratefully, as he contemplated the sea and the sky.

I gave him his favourite sweets to suck on. 'Oh,' he said with deep gratitude, 'these are good.'

We remained there in the afternoon sun, watching the tide slowly creep up until I realised he had gone to sleep and it was time to go back.

'Dear,' he whispered again, 'it is good to see you.'

The next day, when I visited, he was asleep on the bed and I didn't want to disturb him. I left and went to my faraway home. I never saw him alive again. As I travelled home, he died.

I did see him one more time, lying in his coffin. I found it very reassuring to sit next to the body and talk to him. I don't get to see many dead bodies. They are so cold, so very dead, and you can really tell the light has gone out.

I had reached the point where it was all too overwhelming for me, so I set out on a pilgrimage.

I would leave Australia and go far away, to England, Scotland, India and New Zealand. Places I loved and where I knew I could hide and heal. I was ashamed of my inability to cope and was useless at all the paperwork and administration I faced at work. I couldn't see the point. I couldn't accept the sympathy of friends and the pity of colleagues. I wanted to leave behind pain and to find new understandings to ease my aching heart. I knew that, in order to go forward, I would, I *had*, to go back. I would, inevitably, have to address everything in the past that I had hoped to leave behind. This would happen now that everything had been tossed up.

These endings were my beginning.

CHAPTER ONE

Here be dragons

In olden days, when maps were drawn and the cartographers didn't know what was in the empty space, they would write 'Here Be Dragons' to signify unknown and possibly dangerous territory. Death is like that for many of us—unknown and dangerous territory. It is unmapped. We don't know the way and we don't know what we might encounter. We are afraid of dragons.

One way, I think, to temper your encounter with the dragon of death is to sit with the body of the deceased. I have found it unexpectedly consoling and reassuring.

When my twin brother died I did not think I could face life with any kind of competence ever again. I went to see his body. I looked at his strangely made-up and composed face. I touched him. He was very cold. My body felt shrivelled up, clenched with pain, anger, despair.

I pulled up a chair next to him and began to talk through my tears, asking how he could leave me, how was I to live without him. And as I sat there the strangest thing happened. A deep and comprehensive sweetness came from him directly into my heart. The longer I sat, the stronger the sensation became. The distress and pain subsided in the face of this flow of love. I knew, in my twinly heart, that he was telling me he was fine and happy, and to not worry anymore; that I was to trust he was all right. He had been unhappy for so long, but was no longer in pain and burdened by misery. After that I could manage the funeral, the eulogy, the tea and sandwiches. I could manage it all, as I felt his presence alongside.

I feel it still.

My carefully constructed map of everyday life had reached unknown territory, but I had found clarity in that strange place of pain. The fearful dragon of death lay quietly at my feet, tail curled alongside. I received strength from an unexpected place. Sitting next to him, my twin had given me a message of love that was palpable, that changed the jagged edge of pain into a keenness of knowing and the beginnings of understanding.

A few months later, I was looking at my father's body. He was laid out in the waistcoat knitted for him by his beloved wife, my stepmother (a kiss in every stitch), wearing his Masonic badge proudly stating a fifty-year membership. I patted his bony hands. Here, the pain was not so raw. After all, he was ninety-three. I was able to talk to him and say private farewells to the man who terrorised my childhood. Once quick to anger, he had become faded and pathetic in old age.

Sitting by the body offers strange, unexpected consolation. It gives an opportunity to talk and know the person is really gone—that he or she hasn't merely disappeared. Different rituals are observed. Some sit in vigil, some wash and dress the body. Candles are lit, music is played. It allows you to see that the life spirit has left the body; the animating force is extinguished.

It can have its moments. An Irish friend told me about sitting with his many sisters and brothers as his father lay in his coffin, in the parlour of their Belfast home. They laughed and cried, smoked, drank tea and Guinness and reminisced. At one stage one of their father's eyes opened ever so slightly. A wee slit appeared, which disconcerted the sitters. The eldest sister, always the leader, popped her cigarette in her mouth, leaned over and pressed it shut again, saying, 'There, now,' and the conversation, stalled into brief, appalled silence, resumed.

Perhaps it is unwise to assume that all dragons are harmful. 'Here Be Dragons' signals the unknown, and although that's scary, that's where there is the most to discover. I had dreaded the death of my brother for many years, knowing the pain it would bring. Yet in that unknown place he gave me an irreplaceable gift, one that holds still and strong in my battered, beating heart. There can be consolation in dark places.

I have a friend in New Zealand who has survived two rounds of cancer as well as the Christchurch earthquakes. As a musician and artist she painted and sang her way through the numerous losses— her health, her hair, her city. She lives high on the Port Hills, looking across the Canterbury Plains to the dramatic and severe Southern Alps. In winter the mountains march in stunning, snow-clad beauty down the length of the South Island.

She told me that the cancer and the earthquakes both, in their destructive power, had shaken her to her core. 'It's been a gift in a strange way, though,' she said. 'We were settling down in an unquestioned rut. We knew we must make changes, but we were waiting—and for what? A better moment? Now I know with certainty that there is no better moment. This is it. This is all I have—and it's wonderful. No running ahead, no looking back.'

Eighteenth-century English poet Elizabeth Barrett Browning wrote:

> God answers sharp and sudden
> On some prayers,
> And thrusts the things we
> have prayed for in our face,
> A gauntlet with a gift in it.

The poet is telling us that there is *always* something we need or want, hidden in something unwanted, unbidden. A gauntlet, that medieval armoured glove used to issue a challenge to combat, hence the phrase 'to throw down the gauntlet', is symbolic of what happens when death and upset arrive suddenly and forcefully in our lives. We are issued a challenge, one that can feel unbearable, unreasonable and hateful. Yet the challenge is that we must survive and, even more if possible, survive to be richer and stronger. Our loss never leaves and maybe, just maybe, we gain in ways we never knew would nourish our wounded hearts.

In Christchurch the dragon had shifted in its sleep and shaken the city down. Lives were tossed into the air, houses tumbled down, people died. For me also, a great disruption had sent me spinning, but, like my friend, the complex gift of loss and grief had precipitated all kinds of knowing and understandings.

CHAPTER TWO

A beetle trapped in amber

So we beat on, boats against the current,
borne back ceaselessly into the past.

F Scott Fitzgerald

I am fascinated by the fossils of creatures trapped in amber. Some of them have been preserved for millions of years. The insects, caught in the dripping sap of ancient trees, float eternally in their amber prison. When people die it is as if they too are trapped in amber. Some remain forever romantic, unsullied and young. Kurt Cobain, the grunge-rock musician from Seattle, who died in an apparent suicide in 1994, and Heath Ledger, the Australian actor who accidentally overdosed in New York in 2008, are both men who had achieved great artistic success and died in their late twenties.

Troubled and irreverent, Cobain gave us the song 'Smells like Teen Spirit', and, for many, Ledger will always be the robust, complicated cowboy of the film *Brokeback Mountain*.

These icons remain frozen, ageless, unsullied by any further ravages of life. It happens in our personal lives also. The brother of a friend of mine contracted HIV/AIDS in his youthful twenties. His decline was distressing and relentless. He became blind, thin and weak and, one bleak morning, as we watched helplessly, he took his last painful breath.

My friend has a photo of his brother from his early days of health and beauty, lying asleep on a couch. This photo has sat on a shelf in every one of the houses he has lived in. The brother sleeps on, in his amber kingdom. On my dressing table is a black-and-white photo of my mother. She died nearly forty years ago and this is the last photo ever taken of her. She is at my sister's wedding, smiling, with a smart hairdo, a brand-new frock, wearing a corsage and her own mother's locket. She is a shadowy memory for me now, frozen in time.

Sometimes the dead one becomes an object of veneration, sanctified and mythologised, which makes it hard to see them in any other way. It may be there comes a time, perhaps a safe distance away from sorrow, when it's possible to see flaws of the deceased person as well as strengths, to admit loss and wear the scars less visibly, less painfully. For others the story becomes entrenched and the myth controls their life.

Take, for example, Miss Havisham, from the Charles Dickens novel *Great Expectations*. She was jilted on her wedding day and sat for years after, like a cadaverous waxwork, in a ruined wedding dress. The breakfast feast and wedding cake stood untouched, mouldering, covered in cobwebs on the decaying, once-festive table. All the clocks in her crumbling mansion were stopped at twenty minutes to nine, the exact time she received a letter saying her marriage was no more. Overcome by grief and loss, she was frozen in time, trapped by her sorrow, shame and humiliation, unable to move, a tragic figure.

Jane was widowed early in her marriage. Her husband had died on a distant battlefront and there had been a hero's funeral for him back on Australian soil. Fine words were spoken, politicians expressed their sadness, flags were lowered and bugles heard. It was all profound and moving. She struggled to readjust her life and her expectations, and to bring up three young children.

After a period of time, things settled down. The hovering friends and family relaxed, the children went to school and there was a general feeling Jane had reached a place of safety. Then she acquired a suitor. Aha, her friends thought, perfect! A father for those children and no more loneliness. But Jane was unable to find anyone who could live up to the saintly perfection of her husband. He remained petrified, like a beetle in amber. She vigorously maintained his sacred memory, backed up by photos and framed medals spread about the house. She referred to him constantly. The suitor left. Others came and went, but none could compete with a ghost. Jane kept talking about her long-lost husband. She stayed frozen, like Miss Havisham.

Memory is not always sacred and reverent. Loss can keep us frozen in a place of resentment or pain. It can continue to wound. Sally had been treated very badly by her lover. Infidelity and abuse were rife and she suffered greatly. After time, and with help, she managed to leave him and retrieve a semblance of a normal life. However, the drama of the relationship and the injury and insult lived on in the story she would tell anyone, given the slightest opportunity. Eventually it drove friendship away as people tired of her singing the same song, over and over. Here the myth served her unmoving sorrow and kept her in darkness. It was as if she in some way enjoyed the thought of herself as a tragic, wounded figure.

Loss can fix your position in life. When I looked around there was evidence of frozenness everywhere. Certainly, the death of my mother in a car accident when I was a young woman had changed the course of my life and defined me for a good long time. Eventually, though, I had moved on. I grew up enough to understand that she was an ordinary woman, doing her best to make her way through a troubled marriage, rather than someone who had left me too soon. To free her memory, somehow, I had to free myself.

There was a woman I knew who talked constantly about her childhood and her sense of parental abandonment. Her father had left her mother for another woman when she was a young girl. Later, on a skiing holiday with his new family, he died. The woman had adored her absent father and would not accept him to be anything other than wonderful. She remained at odds with her mother, spoiled any new relationships for her and kept his photo in a locket around her neck. He had become one-dimensional and venerated. Part of her remained stuck at seven years old. The frozen daddy had had an impact on every relationship she had, particularly those with men, in her life. She was not free and neither was her father. He remained stuck in the amber prison of her attachment to the grief of her loss.

I thought about the notion of frozenness a great deal, trying to unpick the elements and to understand veneration, attachment and anguish. Even the war memorials all over the country honouring the fallen speak about it. Everyone in adult life carries loss, and how they let it operate in their life impacts on everything. This only serves to underline how sorrow is not neat, tidy and separable; how it can't be dealt with chop-chop, there, that's done, move on; how it echoes down lives, sometimes paralysing people.

The absent heroes and heroines, the lost loves, the sepia photographs, cobweb cakes and the sombre statues of soldiers in dusty squares in every country town tell me that grief and loss walk with us all the time. I can see how we can become frozen in the clutches of grief and then, in time somehow, move to a kinder place of memory where the amber prison is transformed into a poignant memorial.

Miss Havisham, sitting at her table in ruined wedding dress, exemplifies how loss can cripple and keep the past as ruler. The veneration of pop-culture idols and personal heroes also speaks to a simplification of that grief and an unwillingness to accept the responsibility that comes with love, to let another, dead or alive, breathe and move from their amber vessel. As I see it, for us to be freed from grief, we have to free them also.

CHAPTER THREE

Thin Space

There is a mysterious power that pervades
everything. I feel it, though I do not see it. It is this
unseen power that makes itself felt and yet defies
all proof, because it is so unlike all that I perceive
through my senses. It transcends the senses.

Mahatma Gandhi, 1931

The Celts say Heaven and Earth are only ever three feet apart, if we could but see. The term for this liminal space where Heaven and Earth are so close together that the spiritual and natural worlds intersect is Thin Space. Thin Space describes the place where the veil between the worlds is thin and we feel the presence of the Divine. Thin Space can be found in sacred sites, temples and shrines but also in wild and remote places in nature. When we move into Thin Space we become aware of transcendence. The energy shifts, eyesight and hearing become keen, and the trappings of daily life slip away.

Theseus, according to Greek mythology, found his way out of the labyrinth, where he had been sent to slay the Minotaur, by following a thin red thread. When I found myself walking in circles in a maze of grief, I followed a thin red thread of an idea, given to me by a stranger on a plane, and I went far away to the Western Isles of Scotland and the island of Iona. On this island there is magic and mystery in the air. The trees whisper, the ground hums and the sea turns from turquoise to dark green. Sometimes seals can be seen poking their slick black heads above the water. If you are lucky, dolphins will chase your little boat as you cross the sea. Here is Thin Space.

This island has a long and venerable history. St Columba landed here in 563 AD and, with twelve followers, is said to have brought Christianity to Scotland and the British Isles. It is holy: a centre for monasticism and retreat for over 400 years. The island has stone Celtic crosses, chapels, Iona Abbey and ancient burial grounds for Scottish and Irish kings. Some suggest that *The Book of Kells*, the famous and historic illuminated Latin manuscript of the four Gospels of the New Testament, was written here.

It is a centre for ecumenical community, drawing men and women from all traditions and life experiences to its sacred heart. Iona Abbey is large, with cloisters and, on display, an uncomfortable-looking piece of stone that was, so the sign said, St Columba's pillow. People go there on pilgrimage, chasing the sensation of holiness that permeates the soft Scottish air. Occasionally, a cruise ship navigates to the island and disgorges a group of camera-laden, brightly dressed tourists with sensible shoes and loud voices. Somehow it seems as if the island retreats a little when they are there.

As I walked on Iona I saw a rickety wooden sign and followed an indistinct path to the top of a hill. Here I found a circle of peaty dark water glimmering underneath a big grey rock. In the distance I could see smudges of islands floating on the ocean and the clouds changing and moving in a slate-grey sky. I thought, Is this the place I was told about months ago in a bar in sunny Australia—the well of eternal life?

I looked around. On the beach below I could see people walking, made tiny by the distance. I looked at the well. Floating in it were three crosses, woven from reeds, and, curiously, an apple. I looked around again. I was completely alone. I took all my clothes off and waded into the soft dark water, plunged my head under and floated in the murky depths. Then I climbed out and put my clothes back on my damp body. I walked down the hill, humming.

The afternoon felt charged with magic. I talked with no one. I was invisible. The abbey was empty and still. In the chapel three candles glowed on a low wooden table covered with a coarse white cloth. I walked to the ruined nunnery and sat on a bench, leaning my back against a rough stone wall. Flowering grasses rattled in the breeze and the air shimmered. I felt empty, light and floating. I could hear the tinkling sound of boats and the occasional lowing of a cow. I sat still for a long time in the late afternoon sun, my mind washed clear.

Thin Space also describes that altered condition of the grieving person. In her book *The Year of Magical Thinking*, American writer Joan Didion refers to the strange state of discombobulation that overtook her the year her husband died and her daughter went into a coma: how she could remember only strange things, like being in the hospital in her slippers or making decisions about food. Didion knew she must have eaten, but she couldn't describe a single meal. She was both floating and acutely alert, only not to everyday concerns.

Emily Post, the American doyenne of manners, in her 1922 book on etiquette, talks of the 'genuine affliction' that occurs in the grief state. I like the phrase 'genuine affliction'. It gives gravitas to the state of suspended and ongoing shock that is grief. 'No one,' Post explains, 'can under such circumstances be normal.' This is the altered space, the way of being that describes how in times of grief and loss, we walk with different awareness in the world. As Post puts it: 'At no time does solemnity so possess our souls as when we stand deserted at the brink of darkness into which our loved one has gone.' Confusing and disorientating, it can also be empowering. In that Thin Space of affliction comes clarity, unfettered by daily expectation and obligation. Decisions once prevaricated over are taken. Priorities, relationships are sharply rearranged.

Post and her writing on etiquette offer much to help with navigation of Thin Space. It is at times like these that etiquette is most useful, as the rituals and observances offer a 'vital and real' service when everything else seems rocky and unreliable.

> *It is the time-worn servitor, Etiquette, who draws the shades, who muffles the bell, who keeps the house quiet, who hushes voices and footsteps and sudden noises; who stands between well-meaning and importunate outsiders and the retirement of the bereaved; who decrees that the last rites shall be performed smoothly and with beauty and gravity, so that the poignancy of grief may in so far as possible be assuaged.*
>
> Emily Post, *Etiquette*

I took my pilgrimage to Iona after my twin died. Two weeks before I left, my father died, and it was in that maelstrom of stripped defences that I set out across the world. My heart was tipped empty as I flew across the oceans. I was lacking courage. I went because I couldn't stay where I was. I felt useless, good for nothing.

Before I left Australia I looked for a hotel to stay in overnight in Singapore. I found one called the New Happy and I took it as a sign. That'll do me, I thought. The hotel was tall and narrow, and in the tiny foyer a severe young woman with purple hair and black nails looked surprised to see me. Sulky young women walked past with men in tow. My room had a double bed and a tiny bathroom. Beside the bed was a box of tissues and two shower caps.

I had booked myself into a short-stay love hotel. Perfect. I laughed. It was clean enough and when I walked the streets I found good food. But I fled in the early hours of the morning and boarded the plane to London. From there I caught two trains, a ferry, a bus and small boat on a trip that took all day to reach the Inner Hebrides and the island of Erraid, next to Iona, where I would begin the process of recuperation.

On Erraid I followed daily rituals that gave me a semblance of structure in an uncertain time. The tiny community I stayed with asked that I contribute by way of allotted tasks, such as washing up, sweeping, working in the garden. The rest was up to me. I could join in activities as I wished. I chose to go on a walk to see an ancient giant oak tree that had fallen and now grew sideways across a valley. This meant walking off the island when the tide was out, across the Narrows and up to a squelchy heath covered in blooming heather.

For two hours I trekked, following carefully the steps of the person in front of me, trying not to slip into bogs. There were five of us. We plodded across the island in silence to a secret place where the extraordinary oak grew. It filled the whole valley with its mossy branches and dripping solemnity. Peace came dropping slow, as Yeats described in his poem 'The Lake Isle of Innisfree', and was immense, consoling and restorative. We sat under the ancient sideways tree and ate bread baked that morning.

Distance from home and the observances of the island community's rituals all helped me stumble through the Thin Space that was part of the recovery from the affliction of grief.

One ritual that can help in a time of grief is to make a shrine or some kind of remembrance place to a loved one. My friend Martin was bereft when his partner committed suicide. His pain was immense. He was wracked with guilt and confusion for many years afterwards. Although he managed to stumble his way back into working life, the story of her death was never very far away and when he drank, which was often, he would talk about her, endlessly working and reworking the story of her death. He had exhausted the patience of his friends and the kindness of his family. 'Move on,' they would exhort. 'Let it go.'

But he was stuck. One day we were sitting in his overgrown and neglected garden. It was late summer and the sky was bleached white. I could hear the sea in the distance and the steady hum and whir of cicadas. He had started mowing the lawn and stopped halfway to sit on his chair and have a smoke. I looked around. The house needed painting. Piles of wood stood knee-high in grass, pots toppled sideways and tools lay rusting in the open door of a dark and cobwebby shed. In the corner, under some straggly trees, was the grave of his much-loved cat, marked by a wooden cross.

He began to talk about his lost love and I could feel a familiar irritation rise in me. I thought of the poet Mary Oliver's words: 'Someone I loved once gave me a box full of darkness. It took me years to understand that this, too, was a gift.'

'Why don't you make a shrine for her?' I suggested. 'You could make a place in the garden, plant her favourite flower and decorate it. You have one for your cat Freckles, why not one for her?'

He pulled on his cigarette and considered the matter. 'Yes,' he said slowly, 'I could do that.'

I pressed on. 'Think of it this way. You have so many thoughts about her in your head; why not make a place where you can put them? You can greet her every day, talk to her and get off the painful treadmill of rehashing her death and your role in it. It won't explain it but it might help ease your sorrow.'

At that point he got up and went into the house. I worried I had interfered too much, but he came back with a necklace of semi-precious stones. He sat heavily on the faded wooden chair.

'I could put this in the ground for her,' he said. 'I was going to give it to her and I never had the chance. I can't give it away and it has been sitting there on the shelf ever since the night she died.'

I left him then, sitting, smoking and mulling things over. I went to the beach of black sand, driftwood and crashing waves. Bluebottle jellyfish littered the shoreline. Later, as the afternoon drew on and shadows lengthened, I dropped in on my way home. He was busy. He had finished the mowing and had cleared out the weeds under the feijoa tree.

'I'm making a place for her to rest in my garden,' he said. His nails were blackened with dirt and digging implements lay nearby. He looked pinker than I had seen him in a while. The miasma, that grey foggy taint that had lingered around him, was dispersed. He offered me a drink but I left him to it. I had my own ghosts to lay to rest.

My friend had been floating in Thin Space for years. The action of building a shrine in his garden in remembrance of his love helped bring him back into the world. He could now, perhaps, begin to recover from the loss, rather than be defined by it.

We inhabit Thin Space when we bear the affliction of grief, what Jung describes as 'legitimate suffering'. We also can seek out Thin Space by going to sacred, overlooked, quiet places, building shrines, diving into holy wells, climbing toward mountain tops and following pilgrim trails. WH Auden says we would rather be ruined than change, but life, as we know, does not stay still, and cataclysmic events, ones we cannot control, mend or understand, take us into Thin Space.

CHAPTER FOUR

Tiny stone stairway

There are insidious aspects to grief that can eat away at us for years, shaping relationships and choices in life. Disappointment is one of these. An unrecognised and undervalued emotion, it can seep throughout our lives, influencing the way we operate, the way we interact. It can surface in many ways, like becoming aware that the dream you had is not going to materialise or that the person you love or loved is not who you thought.

Susie fell pregnant and was told she was having twins. After some initial adjustment, her excitement built, and she and her husband, Tom, started preparing the house for the new arrivals. They bought two of everything and two baby carriers were installed in the family car.

Susie had planned a home birth and prepared carefully for the joyous event. The fridge was stocked, tiny baby clothes were washed, vitamins taken and prenatal classes attended. Her mother hovered anxiously. Tom mowed the lawn. The day came and Susie went into labour. Eventually, a child was delivered. Some time passed and the second baby seemed reluctant to arrive.

Fears escalated. The atmosphere changed. An investigation revealed that there was no other baby and, in fact, there never had been. There had been a misdiagnosis. Somehow, in a fuzzy ultrasound picture, two backbones had been identified and one muffled heartbeat translated as two. It was very confusing.

The joy of a safe delivery had been tainted. Susie was faced with the bewildering emotion of unjustifiable disappointment. I went to see her. Her husband was out at the car removing the extra baby carrier. A twin stroller sat forlornly in the hall. I had brought pumpkin and sweet potato soup for her and she ate it cautiously, in tiny spoonfuls. She was fragile, stunned. She wept. The wee baby boy slept blissfully by his mother's side, unaware of the muddle that surrounded his birth.

Susie's marriage suffered from the disappointment of the baby that never was. Tom redoubled his efforts to boost his career as a real-estate agent and spent all available hours reading books on how to sell houses and promote his business. The house became littered with self-help books, magazines about luxury boats, flash apartments and room-styling tips. Susie's natural vivaciousness turned brittle. Her lipstick became brighter and brighter. Her disappointment proved hard to budge. She couldn't stop telling the story of the bungled birth. The baby boy thrived, but it was as if he were second-class to the ghost of his non-existent twin. Then Susie discovered that Tom had started a relationship with a young fitness trainer. Susie put on her red lipstick and drove to the gym. Tom and the lithe trainer were there, sharing smoothies. Susie tipped the table and the milky drinks went all over the floor and onto the designer gym shoes and bags.

'I will never forgive you for the loss of our baby!' she hissed.

'There was no baby,' said Tom sadly, 'no baby at all. You have to let it go.'

But Susie was gone by then, driving ferociously back to her house and her sleeping son. Nursing her disappointment and loss, she took up gin drinking in a determined way. People pointed out that she still had a lovely baby boy and had nothing to grieve about. After all, they said, it wasn't as if there really had been another baby.

With nowhere to put her feelings, and no one to talk to, Susie's world closed down. Eventually, Tom came to claim his child. Susie's mother took her to live with her. Her disappointment had caused such deep affliction she never recovered.

In Stratford-upon-Avon in England is the beautiful Church of the Holy Trinity where playwright William Shakespeare is buried. Outside, an ancient tree with rough bark and deep-green foliage has grown in a curious, twisted Z-shape across the creamy stone buttresses. Mossy headstones lean over unevenly in the graveyard and pale stone paths lead away to dappled trails that run alongside the river. Inside, tourists shuffle in a version of quiet, taking zillions of digital photos of the chancel and the altar. Saints in stained-glass windows look down on the bright jackets of murmuring sightseers, jostling around plaques that tell the story of the citizens of Stratford in the 1600s.

Discouraged by the crowd and the dilution of the sacred atmosphere, I went into the wee gift shop and there, hidden behind a spindly rack of postcards, was a small doorway with a sign saying *Prayer Room*. I pushed through and climbed up a precipitously steep, extremely narrow, stone spiral staircase to a smallish room full of grey light. One wall held a window, a half-circle of milky old glass. There were twelve low wooden chairs set into two rows of six, facing each other. The air was quiet and heavy with a history of prayer and meditation. I was alone. I sat down feeling reverent and stilled by the atmosphere. I took out the picture of my brother and held it close. I had been running in my brain for so long, trying to get away from the pain of his death. Here I could simply sit and let it wash around me. There was nowhere to go and nothing to do.

In my journey of grief something kept flickering at the edge of my consciousness. I kept feeling there was something I ought to understand. Was it disappointment? I knew I didn't want to be stuck like Miss Havisham seated at her ruined marriage table, looking at her cobweb cake. I wanted to *really* understand what this meant and it was as if to do that I had to go back into the territory of the past and really look at it. I had to go to places I thought I had left far, far behind—like my fear of my father's temper and my guilt about not being able to save my twin.

I sat in that still, stone room full of milky light and I waited. I wanted some kind of epiphany that would take me into deep and wise understanding. I looked at the photo of my brother. I had grabbed it as I left home and kept it tucked inside my shirt to hold him close. The photo had been taken in India. He is standing in denim shirt and jeans in a rustic room, with a big grin on his face. He looks loose, happy and free. A big speckled snake is draped around his neck, and he is cradling its languid body in his hands. Tears leaked down my face. I sat on the low wooden chairs in that Thin Space until my skin grew cold and my knees protested. No marvellous insight arrived.

My life was riven with disappointment. As a child I remember being completely baffled that my brother and I were not loved and protected properly. That disappointment ran deep. My twin brother was unable to overcome the brutality of his childhood. The distress and grief crippled him, crushed his spirit. He died alone and sad.

I got up and went back down the tiny stone stairway and walked back into Stratford toward my accommodation. Japanese tourists were posing in front of the statue of Shakespeare's Fool at the top of the street. The weather had settled into a damp drizzle. I went into a dimly lit pub and ordered a pastie and beer. Both were lukewarm and unsatisfying—another disappointment. The day receded into early evening and I walked along Sheep Street, looking at bizarre wrought-iron sculptures in the window of the art gallery.

No epiphany then, no blinding intuition. Rather, a deep understanding of the power of disappointment and how that emotion needs to be acknowledged, recognised and valued as important, not to be brushed aside or downplayed. To those who say, 'Never mind—you'll get over it,' I look at them sadly, knowing sometimes you don't. You just plain don't.

CHAPTER FIVE

Tricksters and transformation

In ancient Greece, the story goes that Procrustes was a robber who offered hospitality to travellers on the road to Athens. You would lie in his bed, but in order to fit in it, either you would be stretched or any limb that went over the sides would be chopped off.

Despair can be about seeing what you have allowed to be stretched, chopped off and lost, in order to travel to the place of your dreams. And dreams, they change; they can shift from aspirations to external measures of success and value. The myth tells us what we have sacrificed in order to fit in and also speaks to what we leave behind. The aspirant painter becomes an art teacher. The fisherman works in a tackle shop. The actress becomes a game-show host.

Gina rang in tears. Her back and her head and her heart hurt. She told me how she was turning fifty and how she could see that her life was one blind alley after another. Here she was: no children, no money, no man, no work and no prospect of achieving any of the things she had deemed important. She despaired of her ability to have the energy and optimism to sternly talk herself one more time into keeping going. She was lying on a Procrustean bed of her own creation and finding it severely uncomfortable.

The day before, Mark had visited me and also talked about not knowing what to do next. He felt he was not as strong as he needed to be to keep up his work as a builder. His marriage had ended, his children were far away. He was feeling his aloneness and his lack of material success in the world. I was surprised he was talking to me. Normally, he had the heavily guarded heart of the sensitive man. He echoed Gina's despair (minus the tears) of no longer knowing the way and, when looking back, being able to see only the mistakes and losses.

The definition of despair is an absence of hope. Gina's and Mark's confusion and despair were similar. They were in a crossover period in life, a liminal transition, a time of being on a threshold, in neither one space nor another. These transitions are about considering where we might go and what we might do if we no longer worried about trying to fit into a Procrustean bed—one telling us we had to be a certain way (rich, successful) or one we created ourselves (world-class ballerina, prize-winning yachtsman).

Liminal states and despair can happen at any stage, not only at crossover years. My friend Paul had had his heart badly broken at the age of twenty-two. He was a passionate youth, and he suffered badly when his girlfriend, an intense first love, left him. He couldn't cope with his studies, became suicidal, dropped out of university and went surfing in Indonesia. His parents fretted about him. He came back taller, thinner and still unhappy. The grief of lost love hit him hard. He took labouring jobs and tried to purge his pain through manual labour.

I hadn't seen Paul for some time, keeping up with his story through snatches of information here and there. We bumped into each other at the market. There was a gravitas about him that counter-balanced his sweet youthfulness and appealing surfie bleached good looks. He said he had got over the betrayal that had broken his heart. He was going to finish his degree and think of what to do next. He might do architecture, he wasn't sure. He would now take women carefully. Both he and I laughed. He was young and handsome and I knew it wouldn't be long before someone caught his eye. Phew. Transition navigated. He had been to the borders and found his way back again. I liked the change in him.

Psychologists will tell you that the processes of dissolution, liminality and then reassimilation are stages of spiritual growth. This is, perhaps, slender consolation when you feel stuck in a dark tunnel. There are myths that describe this liminal transition state. It is a time when certainties are gone and there are vulnerabilities. In the confusion a trickster may appear. Mail-order brides become attractive, money is sent to unreliable places in search of winnings that never materialise, or the affected person may become a trickster themselves, perhaps attempting to retain eternal youth with dyed hair, flashy clothes or a succession of younger consorts. Interestingly, in theory, when societies are in transition, tricksters appear and assume positions of power, confusing whole nations—Rasputin, Pol Pot, Stalin and Hitler, for example.

Gina decided to go on a trip to Morocco. Casablanca, Marrakech, Fez, kasbahs and medinas—she was intrigued by the exotic call of North Africa and wanted radical change. While there she became enthralled with a handsome Arabic man. Beds were shared and promises made to the sound of fountains, under mauve-dark skies laden with stars. Enchanted, she sold up and made plans to move there, against all the advice of friends. The trickster was soon revealed to be already married, the money was lost and, last heard, Gina had returned to Australia, was teaching English and living in dismal rented accommodation.

Mark began to drink a lot. He became obsessed with his favourite football team. He bought a big motorbike and fell into a community of men who went on long weekend rides, fundraising for children's charities. The world suddenly opened up for him. The shift took him away from the grog and toward a place of community value and recognition. When the group of mates went on big fundraising rides, his role was Mr Fix-it and he was called on regularly to help. His bike was festooned with his footy colours. He was much loved in the group. For both Gina and Mark the Procrustean beds were broken up on the anvil of despair and new identities formed.

In *The Republic* in 360 BC, Plato proposed four arguments against being carried away by adversity and despair. He said:

1. *Things may yet turn out better in the long run*
2. *Anguish doesn't change the future*
3. *Human affairs are not significant*
4. *Anguish prevents healing*

He summed up by saying that the right attitude toward adversity is acceptance, as one accepts the outcome of a roll of the dice.

The cool detachment of Greek philosophy possibly offers insight down the ages. We despair, we are consumed by anguish, and eventually we recover to find ourselves in a place hitherto unknown to us, one we may not have ever considered had our world not been tipped upside down. The deeper our despair, the longer it can take.

Plato's offering that human affairs are not significant speaks to a deeper understanding and reconciliation with the world, one that asks for a huge degree of acceptance. This is in line with his roll-of-a-dice theory. These aphorisms, although noble, are hard to digest when despair cuts a deep swathe through life.

When I read the aphorisms I thought about a grave I had seen in the Bolton Street Cemetery in Wellington, New Zealand. It is for the children of the Wallace family. Five of the children, aged between three and eleven, died between 5 and 24 May 1865. That's just less than three weeks. The sixth and remaining child died three months later. The cause of death, scarlet fever, is inscribed at the bottom of the gravestone along with a passage from the King James Bible: 'Suffer little children to come unto me, and forbid them not, for of such is the Kingdom of God.' The memorial is enough to make you go home and count your blessings.

I was not convinced that the Wallace parents, who lived on until their seventies, would have been sanguine enough, in the face of such devastating loss, to think of this as a roll of the dice. They were, like us, not alone with their tragedy. Despair stalks us all. No one escapes. Our task, in despair, is to meet our shadows, lay to rest shattered or outdated dreams, seed new ones. The path is instinctual and we stumble. The weaving and unweaving of self hold the seeds of a new way of being and knowing.

CHAPTER SIX

Cement sacks and anger

Alone we are born
And die alone;
Yet see the red-gold cirrus
Over snow-mountain shine.

Upon the upland road
Ride easy, stranger:
Surrender to the sky
Your heart of anger.

James K Baxter, 'High Country Weather'

I was talking to a friend of mine. She is a com-posed, competent young woman, a counsellor working in Social Services, committed to her community. I wanted to discuss the notion that it's possible to be consumed by grief and loss. This phrase describes that moment when it all becomes too much to bear and craziness overtakes the brain. The pain can be so extreme that some are driven to incomprehensible acts of madness: this is when people drive into dams with their children in the car, or dangle them over bridges, when murders and suicides are committed.

I told her about William James Mudie Larnach. His story is one of grand passion and grief, and it dominates the history of Dunedin, in the south of the South Island of New Zealand. Larnach was born in New South Wales in 1833. He was an early colonial character, who had a life writ large. He made a career in banking in the Australian goldfields (his equipment then was a dog, a gun and strongboxes). He took up the job of managing Dunedin's Bank of Otago in 1867. His brilliant career saw him run a merchant empire and become a cabinet minister.

Larnach built a splendid mansion on the peninsula beyond the city. Known as Larnach Castle, it took 200 men three years to build in a time when marble came from Italy and glass from Venice—all by ship. He married three times. His first wife had six children and died at the age of thirty-eight. He married his wife's half-sister and she too died at thirty-eight. He then married a much younger woman. His favourite daughter died of typhoid.

He went to Wellington in the North Island on parliamentary business for a month, and while he was away, he became aware that his son and his third wife had fallen in love. He returned to Dunedin and rode his horse into the city, a trip of some 20 miles, went into the parliament house and shot himself in the head.

I thought about that long and determined trip into the city and how he would have been consumed by grief and rage. His loss would have been pounding on his heart.

When I told my young friend this story, she was adamant that everyone has a choice about how much they let their emotions engulf them.

I blinked. 'Aren't there times in life,' I asked her, 'when emotions simply overtake good sense?'

'Everyone has a choice about how much they let that happen,' she said firmly.

I looked around at her immaculate office and thought bitterly, She thinks life is something you can control, you can organise.

I know only too well that there are times when grief becomes overwhelming and life appears too hard to bear. I also know that some people are simply incapable of managing those raging emotions, that they buckle under the weight of the pain. They are inhabited so completely by grief that they are no longer able to marshal any vestige of sense.

And yet my young friend may have a point.

High in the Himalayas, on my pilgrimage, I climbed up a rocky path and scrambled over giant boulders to get to a cave where a Tibetan nun lived. The air was bright and cool. Tibetan prayer flags decorated the trees. In the distance floated snowy mountain tops. We stopped at a tiny hut where I lit 108 butter candles and uttered a prayer for my twin. That is a sacred number in Buddhism that supposedly represents the 108 feelings. My companion, a Tibetan shaman, chanted. Incense filled the air and bells tinkled. Then we made our way further across the tricky terrain to the cave.

As caves go, this was quite good. It had a door, walls and a window—but it was still a cave. No electricity and a large rocky outcrop for bumping your head on. The nun, dressed in maroon robes, had a shaved head, nut-brown skin and strong hands. She offered tea. I accepted humbly and listened to her story, as told to my companion.

She said that she was made to carry cement sacks up a hill by the Chinese invaders of her home country, Tibet. She had to crawl across concrete floors as she washed them. As a result her knees and her back were permanently wrecked. Her message was simple: be grateful.

This struck me forcibly, when I thought of the complaints I would hear back home about not being able to get a park close to the shops or having to share office space. It put things into perspective. The nun may have been consumed by grief and rage at the injustice of her situation, but she had somehow translated it into a perspective that enriched her and those around her. I looked around at the cave. The small stove sputtered as she offered us some greasy-looking biscuits. A thin film of condensation was collecting on the rocky edges above a picture of the Dalai Lama. When I looked up, she was looking at me and smiling. 'Be grateful,' she repeated.

I gave her a cushion that I had carried up the mountain. She was well pleased. Grateful. Could Larnach have been able to transform his rage and sorrow into gratitude? Could that painful long ride into the city by horse, knowing he was going to blow his brains out, have been different? The seething black rage and despair that drove him was born of such intense grief that he was overwhelmed.

I remembered hearing on the radio a man who talked about being attacked by a shark in Sydney Harbour. The interviewer appeared keen to hear about how horrible the event was and how terrifying sharks are. The man refused to be drawn. He explained that, although he had lost an arm and a limb in the attack, he found it had created a whole new life for him, one that he could never have predicted and which offered him a great deal. These days he travels the world, advocating for shark conservation. He has a new job, a new relationship and a transformed outlook on life.

A few months after our first meeting, I went back to visit my young social-worker friend. She had been told she had inoperable lung cancer and six months to live. When I visited her she was sitting in a sunny, comfortable room with vases of flowers, nice art on the wall, papers and books lying about, and a brown and white dog with its nose pressed against the glass doors into the garden, yapping.

'The nurse who just came had the nerve to tell me this was a valuable learning experience,' she snapped, as she shifted irritably on the couch. 'Shut up!' she yelled at the dog, who paused only briefly.

'I am furious about this. I never even bloody smoked. I eat well and I exercise. I do good things. If anyone dares to pity me I won't be responsible for my actions. It's bad enough to lose all privacy and independence along with having to be grateful for kindnesses and to smile.

'Acceptance? Don't make me laugh. So I have to become all sublime and accept that I will never have children, never live to a ripe old age? I am filled with murderous rage! I could have slammed that righteous do-good nurse up against the wall! This is a time about loss upon loss upon loss. The only gain I have is clarity. I know very well what I want and what I don't have time for.' She sighed and a look of great sadness crossed her face.

The dog kept yapping while I made tea and the conversation turned to the safer zone of workplace gossip. I was uneasy next to her anger and yet felt compelled to respect it. I had nothing to offer and didn't want to be trite. The comfortless advice of sages was no good here. I couldn't know how she felt. Her rage seemed reasonable to me in an unreasonable situation. I longed to smack the dog.

Betrayals by the body, betrayals of the heart, earthquakes, shark attacks and savage losses all tip us into shock. Grief and the attendant sorrows can mutate into rage and despair. Nothing, nothing at all, is neat in the wild landscape of grief.

The elements needed to traverse through grief and rage into gratitude and transformation are different for everyone. Spiritual consolations, a resilient character and time must help. Brenda Walker, an Australian writer, suggests that you can live through just about anything and will eventually float to the surface of terrible turbulence. I didn't dare say that to my friend, trapped by a cruel diagnosis in a sunny room with a yapping dog at the door. I thought about our earlier discussion and her dispassionate appraisal of the tumult of rage and grief. She was barely hanging on. The only tool I had at hand, and it felt barely adequate, was tea.

CHAPTER SEVEN

Donkeys in the dust

Donkeys are sociable creatures. They like company and should never be kept on their own. I learned about them when I visited Bess at her place in the country. She has a few donkeys there, some of them rescued. They are playful, gentle, devoted and affectionate. I never knew what a good friend a donkey could be.

Bess became a widow in her thirties, when her husband was killed by a car as he was crossing the road. They had two children. Recovering, Bess focussed on her family and the work of re-establishing herself as an independent woman, disentangling herself from all the ties of her once married life. She told me a story about the curious status conferred on her as a widow.

'It's kind of like my pain was respectable,' she said. 'I was treated carefully. The women in the suburb where I was living brought me meals, but I couldn't engage with their kid-glove kindness. They hovered. All the time they were talking to me, I felt like I was behind a pane of glass, watching.

'I didn't really think about the status of marriage and now that it's gone, it's as if nobody quite knew how or where to place me. When I went to parties the men treated me with interest and the women with suspicion. It was uncomfortable. So I didn't go out.

'I would go to the pool with the kids and all I could see were happy families everywhere, so I stopped doing that. For a time a few men—husbands of women I knew—came around to help with house maintenance, but I stopped that too. It became too difficult. The women didn't like it. Even though they said it was okay, it wasn't.'

Bess moved. She packed up the house and went north to live in a community with friends from her university days. She took up permaculture and sent her children to the local country school. When I visited her, the kids were setting out with a rag-tag mob of children from the community to play down at the creek. They looked cheerfully unkempt, with unbrushed hair, bare feet and big grins. They waved to us as we sat on the verandah, drinking tea and watching the chooks scratch around.

'The pane of glass sensation didn't leave until after I moved away,' Bess said. 'Until then I was still being obedient to a world where I no longer belonged. I couldn't make myself care, and I was becoming resentful of the need to thank everyone all the time. Gratitude is a horrible burden. I would sit at night and drink. I had to go.'

Bess looked different. The stain of grief had lifted. She was wearing sturdy boots, jeans and a flannel shirt. Her hands were toughened-up, working hands. Her hair was tied back loosely. When she laughed, I realised I hadn't seen her do that for months on end.

'The community here is a mash-up,' she said. 'Families, singles, gays, lots of kids. There's the usual power struggles, of course. Same loneliness, more possibility.' Then she added, 'You know, it was the donkeys that brought me out from behind the pane of glass. Every day I feed and talk with them. They are loyal, loving and funny. I adore them. They brought me back into the light. They are the best medicine I know.'

She laughed, adding, 'Everyone should have a donkey.'

I left her then, in her house made out of recycled timber and reclaimed leadlight windows. There were two friendly and curious donkeys by the gate. I scratched their ears, looking back at the place—the grass that needed cutting, the chooks, wheelbarrow, gardening tools and an unravelled hose. Clemency, then, in the messy, lived-in, unclaimed places.

Then there is self-imposed alienation.

Greg was very angry when his wife left him. His anger amplified when she remarried. That the new husband had money compounded his humiliation and distress. His visits with his children were strained. The children had toys, holidays and technology he could not afford. This incensed him.

He stayed hostile and resistant, and withdrew further and further, discouraging offers of contact and support. Friends talked about him with concern. While they sensed his anguish, his unwelcoming attitude kept everyone at bay. The children began to dislike visiting him, complaining that he would keep them inside and not let them socialise. The moment they were old enough to exercise their will, they refused to see him anymore.

Greg lost his job. He became steadily withdrawn, brooding. A recluse. His self-constructed fortress of forsakenness was both impenetrable and difficult for his children to bear. They left him alone. He had embarked on an internal journey to a wasteland of pain.

It is difficult for those who care about someone to watch them walk inexorably toward that bleak and sorrowful desolation. The distress is apparent, yet the solid wall of self-protecting alienation keeps everyone away. CS Lewis wrote, when his wife died, that no one had told him grief felt so much like fear. Anger, pain and fear are all part of the deal with grief. Greg's grief and anger was visited on all those who cared about him. Freud said we are never so defenceless against suffering as when we love. Addictions, alienations, citadels of pain—it was all strong stuff.

Time spent with donkeys in the dirt was my kind of redemption. I wished I could send some donkeys up to Greg to lead him out of his fortress. Those humble fellows might be the only ones that could walk past all the barriers and fetch him, bring him back to us. But his fierce and determined attachment to his pain and resolute sense of victimhood had made him unapproachable.

I don't know why some people can keep travelling through the landscape of grief and some stay stuck. Writer and mythologist Joseph Campbell says,

'It is by going down into the abyss that we recover the treasures of life. Where you stumble, there lies your treasure.' You could say it takes courage or resilience or a kind of bloody-mindedness to not be beaten down. I don't think it's that simple, though. For some people their suffering sits so heavily in their hearts that the distress they feel locks them out of any possibility of recovery and redemption. They stay trapped in the wastelands, and all around can only watch powerlessly, with great sadness. Bess had donkeys to bring her back, release her from the grip of grief and abandonment. Greg was holding on tight. Like the story of alcoholism and addiction, those who loved looked on with fear and sorrow, helpless, as a life was directed relentlessly into the dark.

CHAPTER EIGHT

Remember to indicate

I was in the car with my old friend Cara. In the last year, by slow and painful degrees, her mother had succumbed to illness and passed away. Cara is a robust, practical type. A no-nonsense woman. She had had to deal with practicalities within her family as they wrestled over wills, ashes and the leftover business of their mother's life. Cara was well equipped for that, but less equipped for the sibling tug of war and argument about money and possessions.

After the funeral—the tea, sandwiches and brandies with relatives and friends—one of the most challenging tasks of dealing with a death is the clean-up. The disposal of stuff that mattered to someone and now looks like so much, well, stuff. This is what is left behind, what Margaret Gibson, in her book *Objects of the Dead: Mourning and Memory in Everyday Life*, refers to as 'objects of death'. They can cause so much trouble, confusion and angst.

While Cara was sentimental over some of her mother's belongings, her sister wanted to dump the lot. Another family member swept in, retrieved the only objects of monetary value and took them away, asserting that no one really wanted them. Ugly, harsh words were spoken and love was lost at a time when love was needed.

Another friend of mine, well acquainted with the mysteries and passions of death, said, 'You know, it's not greed that makes people behave so strongly and strangely around possessions. It's grief.' I realised it's little surprise that large helpings of wisdom are needed to fully understand that, when I considered the havoc and emotional chaos that can occur after a death.

Cara and I were chatting about our children, the way old friends do, as I drove her to the airport. Suddenly she began to weep for her mother. I drove, she wept. Eventually, her tears subsided and she got ready to negotiate the numerous gates that are part of airport travel. She was fine to do it. That is how it is—one moment you're fine and then a wave catches you and knocks you sideways. Your heart clenches in pain. You stagger a little, you weep. Then you go and deal with the practicalities of travel, of shopping centre car parks, electricity bills.

In Wellington, New Zealand, there is a tunnel that leads through a hill on the way to the airport. At the airport end, the road immediately divides and drivers need to make a swift decision to choose left or right. To assist, the roads authority has thoughtfully posted a sign for drivers, saying *Remember to indicate.* This is good advice. Just think how much clearer to negotiate life would be if people indicated their intentions.

In our death-denying society, it is wise to put your house in order while you still have the wit and wherewithal to do so. Others have to clean up after you are gone and often at a time when they are feeling distressed and emotional. So, friends, remember to indicate. Make a will. Get your end-of-life instructions sorted out. There are people who can help you organise and specify your end-of-life preferences, but if you don't prepare, at the end of your life you might find yourself in a position where you cannot express how you want to be cared for and what level of medical intervention you might or might not want.

Fresh from the death of my father and brother, and the harsh reality of packing up their homes, I went to a workshop specialising in Death Directives. It was undoubtedly confronting and yet somehow empowering. We were given questions to consider—all of which were decisions that someone would have to make. For example: what sort of funeral would we want? There are many things to consider, such as cremation or burial, music, prayers, poems, readings, ceremony style, viewing (or not) of remains, washing of the body, vigil, wake, type of coffin and so on.

Some religions make those decisions for you, so this may not be relevant. But there may also be a moment before death to consider. Do you want to have life-prolonging treatment? If so, what sort and for how long? What do you consider a reasonable quality of life? Over the course of the workshop I thought about it and, for me, not being able to read or hear stories would make my life very small.

These are all life-altering decisions you can make, or at least have influence on, that ease the burden of grief for others in a difficult time. Without trying to control from beyond the veil, it is helpful for those left behind if you have remembered to indicate.

For the grieving, loss can be marked by clothing. The manner of our dress offers signals to help us negotiate the exigencies of daily exchange. Surf shorts, tattoos and T-shirts with political slogans all signal the attitude of the wearer. In mourning— and this can and will go on for an unknown length of time—a mourning brooch or a black armband indicates loss and that the carapace of daily life is fractured.

Mourning clothes used to be much more common, even required. In many European and European-influenced countries there was a time around the eighteenth century when there were shops that sold mourning clothes, complete with hushed atmosphere and discreet assistants.

Such garb tells us that someone is in the fragile space of loss and grief. The colours of the clothing are an outward display of inner feelings. Here, say the clothes, I am sad: please understand that I have suffered a loss and am treading a delicate path in the world, and if I look remote, it's not about you; it's because I am in mourning and need time.

The business of mourning in Victorian England was prescribed. When Queen Victoria of England was widowed in 1861, at the age of forty-five, she mourned the loss of her beloved royal consort,

Prince Albert, and wore black mourning dress for forty years. She refused to appear in public for three years. Eventually, her subjects became exasperated and hung a sign on the gates of Buckingham Palace, saying: *These commanding premises to be let or sold in consequence of the late occupants' declining business.*

Queen Victoria's obsession with mourning the loss of her husband had a strong influence on the industry of grief and mourning. At that time, women would wear black, usually crepe (nothing shiny), for a year, moving down to black with a white trim and then, perhaps, to purple as a transition back into the busy world. Jewellery was discreet: a brooch inlaid with the hair of a lost loved one, jet (black) earrings. Men would have black-bordered handkerchiefs and would wear a black armband. Women might wear veils to hide a face saddened with tears.

In some countries the colour of mourning is white. In other cultures people daub themselves with ashes; some observe elaborate rituals of fire and smoke. The main thing is that by wearing mourning clothes or features of mourning dress, we indicate our state. Grief and mourning have no timetable. You may think you are okay and then, suddenly, you know you are not.

After my twin died I tried to go out with friends, but found I offered poor company. I should have known better and stayed home. Then when I felt ready, it would have been good to wear something that indicated I had a tender heart and wasn't quite ready to laugh and carry on with the group. This would have told the world that my quietness didn't need explaining away or oversensitive understanding, just acceptance that I was making my way back into the daily world. Let me sit, my black armband or my jet brooch would say, I am here yet not quite here.

A few months later I met up with Cara in a cafe in inner-city Sydney. A male staffer with a carefully styled beard, tattoos and glowing white teeth was talking behind the counter to a blonde-headed young woman with her back to us. We waited. Cara looked around at the cafe. The tables needed cleaning.

Cara cleared her throat loudly. The waiter stopped the conversation after winking at his companion.

Cara placed our order, adding coolly, 'Could we possibly have a clean table?'

At a signal from the man the woman went and cleaned up a place for us.

'Really,' muttered Cara crossly as we sat down, 'I have had enough of being ignored, overlooked, bullied or trampled on. After all the kerfuffle over Mum's death and the will, I know this for sure. I will make my wishes abundantly clear to all about what I want to happen when I die. I am not going to rely on any assumptions of good manners or reasonable behaviour.'

The blonde girl placed our coffee carefully in front of us. When I looked up I could see she had Down's syndrome. She beamed at us. 'That's my big brother who made your coffee,' she offered. 'He lets me help out sometimes.' She smiled as she moved away.

'Oh,' said Cara. 'See what I mean? Assumptions will get you every time.'

I looked at my friend's tired, ageing, beautiful face. Pinned to her crumpled linen shirt was a beautiful silver brooch with jet inlay. She smiled and touched it.

'This was Mum's,' she said. 'She wore it when Nan died and now I do. I don't know if anyone can read the signal, but it's there, just the same.' As we left the cafe she put twenty dollars in the tip jar.

CHAPTER NINE

Shock, shaman and subterranean ritual

Steve and his wife, Jemma, owned a furniture shop. On one of his buying trips to South-East Asia to gather stock, Steve began a relationship with a young Thai woman. Jemma rarely went on the trips, as they had three children, one of whom was heading toward the challenging final high-school exams. Jemma found out about Steve's relationship in a sadly predictable way—unexplainable charges on a credit card, elevated phone bills.

The realisation that her husband had been unfaithful was brutal and compounded by the age difference. Steve was sixty and the new woman twenty-six. Jemma related how she 'went bonkers' when she found out.

'I wasn't even sure I still liked my husband, but I had assumed we would stay together, stick it out and get past the period of emotional barrenness we were experiencing,' she said. 'I didn't expect him to simply leave. After twenty-five years, it took a week. Poof! Gone! I reeled under the blow. I was hugely overwhelmed by shock. I couldn't believe that the one person I trusted utterly, and had children with, could behave with such callousness and such indifference. I had been discarded like an old shoe. I was furious and I behaved in ways that are unimaginable to me now. I ranted and raved. I threw things. I swore at the woman, saying to her, "Every time you kiss my husband, think of my children's tears!" I was a woman possessed. I think it took me at least a year to begin to make any sense of the extent of the grief, the damage and depth of the injury.'

Dictionary definitions take care to separate emotional and physical shock, the former being classified as 'a feeling of disturbed surprise resulting from a sudden upsetting event', and physical shock as 'an acute medical condition marked by cold, pallid skin, irregular breathing, rapid pulse, and dilated pupils'. Disturbed surprise rather understates the powerful punch of emotional devastation. Deep distress and disbelief can be utterly disabling. Suddenly, familiar emotional structures are gone and a harsh wind rattles the bones.

The shock took its toll on Jemma physically. She lost 13 kilograms in three months. When Steve told her she looked good, she replied tartly, 'There's nothing like grief to shift that unwanted weight.' Steve, on the other hand, was proudly showing off his pretty young wife to all his friends. When the woman became pregnant, Jemma's despair escalated. As Steve thrived and grew prosperous and expansive in his new marriage, Jemma became a raddled, thin chain-smoker, fearful and distrusting.

I bumped into Jemma in India. Haggard with my own shock and still recovering from my brother's death, I had gone there after my journey to Iona. Jemma was staying at the same hotel in New Delhi as me. We went together to eat in a local South Indian restaurant that specialised in South Indian cuisine, *idli* and *masala dosa*. Jemma told me how she had decided that she was no longer going to be the one left behind. Her children had gone to stay with their father for a few months while she went travelling.

'I realised that I had spent the last fifteen years wiping bums, cooking dinners,' she said. 'I was so upset at the injustice of my situation—Steve's comfort, my humiliation. One day my daughter told me how great their father was because he had bought her a new laptop. In that moment I suddenly saw how small my life was. Steve was having a great time and there was me, wailing on and on, so I suggested they go and live with Dad for a while and I took off. I was sick of being pathetic.'

The waiter came over and served us strong coffee, tipping the liquid with big arm gestures, from container to container in an elaborate, stylised ritual. Outside, the traffic droned on under a washed-out Delhi sky. Jemma was still thin and her eyes looked hollow, but she ate with relish, wiping up the last of her food from the stainless-steel serving tray.

In the restaurant was a Tibetan shaman, whom a Buddhist friend had introduced me to at the hotel. He volunteered to come with us when we went to buy some shawls.

'Are you sure you want to come?' I said, used to Western men bored to tears by the thought of women, fabric and shops.

'Oh, yes,' he said cheerfully, 'I love shopping.'

We hurtled along the crowded streets in an auto-rickshaw, dodging people, taxis, animals and diesel fumes, laughing as he told us how he loved chips and that when people asked him questions he told them to ask 'Google Lama'. We spent ages in the shop, caressing the fabrics and getting saturated in a feast of sensual colours, designs and materials. It was glorious.

I didn't see either of them again until a month later when I was in the mountains. There was Jemma, smoking on the tiny adjoining verandah at the hotel in McLeod Ganj. When I said I was going on a small excursion with the shaman, she asked if she could come. Reluctantly, I said yes. I didn't want to hear any more of her stories, but I felt sorry for her still-gaunt figure.

We three went off in a four-wheel drive that carried us high into the Himalayan mountains. The shaman took us to an obscure path and we climbed to a sacred place, a deep cave that held an elaborate shrine, lit Indian-style, with a sputtering fluorescent light. In front of the altar, which was laden with pictures of His Holiness the Dalai Lama and other deities, flowers, candles and religious objects, a dog slowly licked its testicles.

We followed the shaman further into the cave, me holding down my fear of enclosed places, till we came to a dim space, like a secret chamber, right at the end. There he sat down and took out his drum, bells and a thigh bone. He began to chant. A faint light from the altar spilled into the earth-dank space. A Western man walked into the gloom, stooping under the low roof of the cave, and sat with us. I peered across at him. He was tall and thin with lank brown hair, delicate bony hands and a beaky nose. I slowly realised he looked exactly like my twin. The shaman began a sonorous chant. He blew on the thigh bone and rang the bells. I sat mesmerised, held in place by the intonation and the unnerving feeling that my twin was sitting next to me.

Abruptly the light at the altar fizzled out. All was in darkness. The chant swelled. The shaman began to ring the bells loudly and swing the drum. I should have been afraid, but there was no space for that feeling. Notions of time disappeared.

The chant eased to a stop. The light over the altar snapped on. The dog was still there, snoozing under the marigolds and pictures of various gods and goddesses. The Western man shook the shaman's hand and left. Dazed, I got up and we went outside to find there was chai to drink and some soft arrowroot biscuits. Jemma and the shaman came and sat down. No one spoke. The sky and mountains reverberated in the distance. There were several Tibetan monks sitting around, cheerful in their maroon robes, chatting and laughing. Dogs and children skittered about. The part of me that had clenched up tight in shock when I heard my twin had died began to unfurl, ever so slightly.

It takes a long time to recover from the gut-deep impact of shock. I thought of my great-uncle, returned from war, who would sit for hours on the bench at the back verandah, smoking his roll-your-own cigarettes, gazing into the middle distance. We children steered a cautious path around him, not sure how to approach his stern fragility. Only later did I realise he was grappling with shock. I looked over at Jemma, smoking and playing tentatively with the smiling Tibetan children. She had come a long way from the woman who had hurled a brick at her husband's car and roundly cursed a quailing Thai girl.

The trip with the shaman and Jemma had been good medicine. My journey was taking me both into and out of sorrow. I do know that a doppelganger and a sacred cave can't be ordered online and that grief, shock and loss can't be quantified or measured, compared or arranged, solved or sorted out. I was still out of my depth. I looked over. Jemma appeared to be flirting with the shaman. She was laughing at his jokes and leaning toward him. Clearly Jemma was moving on. Shrewd Tibetan monks flicked their eyes toward them and commented to each other. It looked all very cosy.

Good for you, Jemma, I thought. My tea had congealed with arrowroot biscuit crumbs. I put it down, hefted my bag on my shoulders, and went looking for a ride back down the mountain. Time for me, also, to move on.

CHAPTER TEN

Rituals and consolations

When they were young, my children enjoyed a good pet funeral.

We had pets—goldfish, rabbits, guinea pigs and chickens—and from time to time we would find a cold wee body in the bottom of a cage or floating at the top of a tank. A child would report to me, in sepulchral tones, that Fluffy or Widget or Pinkie was dead. This would be the signal for a funeral.

The cardboard inner tube from the toilet paper, an excellent coffin for a guinea pig, would be decorated. We would assemble and the pet would be laid to rest tenderly in the ground.

'Bye, Mother Goose, you were a good guinea pig,' one child would intone while the other scattered flower petals.

We would then proceed to have a jolly good afternoon tea. We all enjoyed the ritual. Sometimes I wondered if the children enjoyed it a little too keenly. A lot of work would be put into a poem celebrating the life of a goldfish. The development of the ceremony, the writing of poems or speeches, the preparation of the body, the digging of the grave, the building of a little marker with the precious pet's name on it—the intentions and mindfulness of all these rituals helped the children mark the passage of death and farewell their pets.

Rituals serve us well as markers and guides. They can be as simple as a regular bedtime story or as involved as a Viking funeral, where the body was placed on a boat, pushed out to sea and then set alight by a burning arrow. Death has many rites. Maori graveyards (*urupa*) have a tap or water at the gate for washing the hands after visiting the dead, to lift the spiritual restrictions (*tapu*). The wearing (or not) of hats at a ceremony, the throwing of dirt onto the coffin and the eulogy are all rituals that help us through the ceremony of death.

I met a woman who declared her intention to never allow her children to have pets, in order to spare them the pain of loss and death. Apart from the sheer effrontery of thinking she could control life's ability to mete out pain, her children would never know the joy of loving and playing with an animal. If grief is the price we pay for love, would any of us wish to be spared the opportunity to know that sweeping, deep, rich feeling of trust and affection?

To attempt to guard against pain is to somehow deny everything life has to offer. I don't wish pain on anyone, least of all my own children, but I would also not wish for them to have untried, untested lives.

A Buddhist friend, Frank, had raging cancer. I visited him in the chemo ward when he was having his treatments. His partner, an artist from Hobart, would sit nearby and consume meat pies and tomato sauce messily while the toxic chemicals dripped into his lover's veins. We would chat quietly. It was quite convivial in that strange room of pain and hope.

After Frank passed away a funeral was held under huge Moreton Bay fig trees near the sea at Byron Bay. A brochure-blue sky pulsated with heat. Tibetan flags flew and vases laden with flamboyant dahlias wobbled in the unevenly mowed grass.

An Australian Buddhist nun dressed in deepest maroon and with a shaved head rang bells and intoned sonorous chants that sounded mystical, moving and full of portent. An eloquent eulogy was given to remind us about how loved our friend was. We all listened respectfully then walked around the cardboard coffin, which had been painted by friends with lotus flowers and a phoenix, and was so beautiful.

We followed the hearse down the dusty road until it pulled away. Then we drifted back into the wooden country hall and had lashings of tea, cakes and sandwiches. Outside, the dahlias wilted in the heat. Flags drooped. People talked and laughed, remembered our friend and felt the sorrow of the loss. Then we went home.

My children would have enjoyed it. They know how to behave at a funeral—when to be sombre, when to laugh, when to eat cakes.

Surely you jest if your aim is to spare children pain. Life is full of loss. Better to equip them with knowledge of the necessary rituals that can help navigate that inevitable and tricky terrain. I know of no one who has had an unblemished life, has got through life unscarred. I know many whose hearts and spirits have eventually recovered and become stronger for an encounter with pain.

Jesse's son died when he was only eighteen. The community was shocked and rallied around the single father. Teenagers decorated the post on the road that the car had run into on that treacherous night. A solemn and heartbreaking funeral was held and most of the country town's residents attended. The priest spoke of the knowledge that none of us gets to escape sorrow and all of us have each other, strapped on the precarious raft of community.

While there were plenty of women willing to step up and comfort Jesse, it was the friendship of his fishing mates that pulled him through. There were many trips out on the water where not much was said, but plenty was expressed. The ritual act of meeting friends on a chilly morning, driving to a jetty, launching a boat then sailing out into the blue to sit for hours in companionable silence provided a pathway for Jesse back into the world.

Being in nature offers consolation in subtle and deep ways—the feel of the sun on skin, of fresh air in the lungs, of spaciousness above and around, the limpid ocean: all bring a sweetness to the soul that cannot be found elsewhere. American philosopher

Henry David Thoreau wrote, 'We need the tonic of wildness.' The ritual of the fishing expedition, the unspoken acceptance and the balm of a big sky all provided Jesse with healing medicine.

Cemeteries are good evidence of the consolations of grief and the manifestations of love. All the graveyards I have visited speak only of tenderness. Sorrow, yes, but always love. I particularly like the Polynesian graves where plastic flowers and brightly coloured windmills jostle for position with mementoes like toy guitars, beer bottles, little cars and footy colours. I admire the austere Protestant markers and marble Catholic mausoleums with angels and cherubs soaring serenely above.

My favourite tombstone honours Mrs Chippy, the cat (male, but the name stuck), who went to Antarctica in the Shackleton expedition of 1914. He was the much-loved pet of Harry McNish, the ship's carpenter. After the *Endurance* foundered in the ice, Shackleton ordered that the cat be shot on the grounds that he would not survive. McNish never forgave him. Mrs Chippy is remembered in sculpture on McNish's grave in the Karori Cemetery in Wellington, New Zealand. He was even represented on a stamp. The ceremony and ritual which commemorate him and McNish's bravery are significant reminders of love and devotion.

Pain and suffering are attendants in life and offer bitter wisdom. They are allies that bring complex gifts: knowledge of grief, awareness of loss. Dealing with these difficult friends is challenging. They hold the tools for emotional resilience and survival. The consolations of grief are not obvious. The gift of heightened awareness of the value of life, of the preciousness of love, the importance of ritual—these are not things that spring to mind when we are sorrowful and desolate with suffering. Yet they wait for us, quietly, as we howl at the moon and scatter ashes off the sides of boats and mountains.

I walked into the kitchen too early one morning after I came back from my travels and there was a bowl of cherries on the table. I had been awake most of the night, worrying about my brother and his sad, lonely death. I was sorrowful and had been scouring my history for any injuries or failures in the relationship I had committed that I could pull up and examine and use to amplify my pain and loss.

The cherries were delicious. I ate them, spitting the pips out into the garden as I sat with the pain and waited for it to ease. I was learning, inch by inch and after all my raging and weeping, that the consolations of life appear in small ways: cups of tea, bowls of cherries, writings on headstones, the friendship of animals and the comfort of rituals.

CHAPTER ELEVEN

Washing and the Oracle

I thought of my brother again today as I was hanging out the washing. It had been raining off and on for over a week and the change in weather was welcome. I love the smell of sun-dried sheets and was hanging them out when my twin came to mind. I could almost see him out of the corner of my eye, grinning as I wrestled with the damp cloth of the quilt cover, trying to spread it out on the line. It's been a year and a half now since Angus died, and I often feel his presence near or beside me. It's always comforting.

As I picked up the washing basket I remembered the day I met the Oracle. It was in the Himalayas at a small and remote town. My shaman friend and I were walking around a sacred lake when we came across a Tibetan family having a picnic. The woman was wearing the traditional black dress with striped apron, a *chupa*. The children wore faded Western T-shirts. A teenage son watched on. The husband was also dressed Tibetan-style, handsome in a worn, tough-life way.

The shaman talked to them for a while as I gazed at the lake and wondered if it was polluted. He rejoined me and we continued on our circumambulation. Each rotation, I was informed, would shave a lifetime or two off my karmic obligations. I would take any blessing I could get.

'That was the Oracle and her family,' the shaman said.

'Really?' I asked, looking back at the family. She looked so ordinary.

'I have arranged for us to see her tomorrow morning,' he said, and we carried on around the lake, increasing our credit with the spiritual world.

The next morning, well before sunrise, fellow traveller Sara, the shaman and I made our way past the sleeping shops and across a rickety bridge to where a guide was waiting with a torch. She took us down tiny alleyways and past small fields till we came to a house where five or six people huddled under shawls in the pre-dawn cool. One of them had brought a small white dog with a bell around its neck. The dog was unable to settle and kept walking up and down the stairs, jingling and jostling the quietly murmuring group. Inside the house a faint light glowed and a strange keening went on and on.

'That's the Oracle going into trance,' whispered the shaman.

It was dark. The dog started worrying a stick and its owner belted it over the ear. It yelped just as the keening, drumming and bells grew louder.

The door opened suddenly and the Oracle's teenage son led the group into a tiny room with pale-green walls of peeling plaster, a low table with a bell, a faded and discoloured mattress, candles, water and a bucket of sand. The group sat, respectfully and quietly, on the floor. Candles flickered. The dog kept walking around, tinkling. Seated cross-legged on the mattress was the Oracle, unrecognisable from the day before. She was now dressed ornately in an outfit of red, gold and green with an elaborate headdress. She was transformed. Her face was changed; she seemed bigger, stranger.

One by one, members of the group shuffled forward on their bottoms to be closest to her. She would feel their limbs, blow through a thin metal tube onto their skin, spit into the sand and chant over their bodies where they indicated or where she detected ailment on their chest, foot, stomach.

One pale-looking girl edged forward. The Oracle felt her pulse, her skin, and stopped.

'She's telling the family to take her to the hospital,' the shaman whispered to me.

The dog kept fussing and one of the seekers rose from the group and threatened it strongly with his walking stick. The dog retreated for a second or two, and then continued his whining and fussing. All the while the Oracle kept chanting and rocking on the mattress.

Sara came forward and lifted her shirt, revealing a bright pink bra. Then she coughed and pointed to her chest. The Oracle placed the tube on her and blew and sucked hard. She suddenly spat a shiny lump of black mucus into her hand. She showed it to my friend and spoke urgently to her.

'She is telling her she has too much black smoke. She must stop,' said the shaman. Sara nodded nervously.

Then it was my turn. I showed the Oracle my bung knee. She placed strong hands on my skin, pushing the kneecap hard, and blew into the tube over the kneecap, chanted and spat.

'Keep warm. Apply warming salve. You have fluid. Do this and it will not get worse,' she told the shaman, who related what she said to me.

I shuffled back obediently. In the hallway, the son played with his mobile phone.

The candle sputtered out and the Oracle collapsed. She seemed to shrink before our eyes. We were hastily ejected from the pale-green room. Outside it was dawn and the mountains were edged in rose pink.

In silence we walked back into the tiny town. A chai shop was open and we sat at the wooden bench and watched the chai wallah make tea in blackened pots over a clay fire. It was strong, smoky and sweet. It was blissful.

'What just happened?' I asked.

Sara and the shaman laughed and we sat in companionable silence, watching as cows, carts and immaculately dressed schoolchildren began to walk along the dirt road.

I did apply a warming salve. My knee didn't get better, but it didn't get worse either. Sara didn't give up smoking, and I don't know if the girl went to the hospital.

At dusk, the shaman and I went around the lake again and walked up to a Tibetan temple. There, in a small room, I lit another 108 candles for my brother. As evening fell, the temple bell rang, incense burned and the shaman chanted. It took a long time and each candle felt singular, important. The events of the day, meeting the Oracle, circling the lake and lighting the candles had lifted my spirit. I realised I had forgotten to ask the Oracle about my broken heart. This told me that the shadow of sadness had eased, and I knew I was nearly ready to return to the day-to-day world.

We walked back to the town in darkness. We could see into people's houses as we passed, families eating and talking at tables holding metal pots of food, their children with plaits and shiny cheeks, sitting on wooden chairs while dogs lay in watchful sleep near the door.

Back home, half a world away from that mystic place, I realised I had travelled far for some kind of healing that began and ended with me, here, hanging out the washing. There's time and there's space, and after a while the pain subsides to a manageable level and you go back to work. I know that my values have permanently shifted. I attend meetings at work, politely listen and know what's important. In my house I have a small metal ship my twin made in his metalwork class at school when he was twelve. I want to be buried with it. I think about getting a tattoo that signifies him.

Like the Oracle said, I didn't get better, and I didn't get worse. I got different.

The sheets swayed in the breeze. It was perfect drying weather. I looked at my washing with a lot of satisfaction. I thought I heard my brother chuckle.

CHAPTER TWELVE

Pilgrim path

The little island seemed to float on the dark lake-waters.
Trees grew on it, and a little hill rose in the middle of
it. It was a mysterious island, lonely and beautiful.
All the children stood and gazed at it, loving it and
longing to go to it. It looked so secret—almost magic.
'Well,' said Jack at last. 'What do you think? Shall
we run away and live on the secret island?'
'Yes!' whispered all the children. 'Let's!'

Enid Blyton, *The Secret Island*

My pilgrimage had taken me over the hills and far away. I met people, heard stories and saw things: seals in the cold waters of the Hebrides, a cave or two in the Himalayas, a sacred well, crowded cities, physic gardens, holy lakes, silent temples and portentous islands.

What did I learn, at great cost to my impatient soul? First, that this was and is a solitary journey. I had asked anyone and everyone to come with me, but all had declined. This was my journey to make. Secondly, that I needed to stop. In India, every lock I encountered proved difficult and needed coaxing. At first I thought that this was a case of poor quality Indian locks, but then I noticed it affected no one else. Others swanned in and out, using the same doorways and locks that had proved uncooperative for me.

Every single time I went to use a lock I was forced to wait, to stand still and, with great patience, get the lock to work. It was enormously irritating. No amount of cursing or urging would speed up my progress. Others laughed at me. I would ask them to unlock the doors and *ta da!* the locks would spring open.

This was not the first time India had given me a lesson. As a young woman I had gone there, nourishing a fantasy about my toughness. But once I arrived, I started to cry. And not gentle, ladylike weeping. Oh no. Loud, heaving, snotty sobbing that would take over my whole body. What's more, it would happen at crowded train or bus stations, in crowded bazaars. I was unable to stem the flow of tears. Crowds of interested bystanders would gather around, staring at me while I sobbed. The tears ceased only once I had accepted it was okay to cry. Same deal, India said to me. Wake up, girlie.

The locks refused to work as long as I hurried them. I understood suddenly how I had been on the run for years, running as fast as I could away from pain or anything I thought might hurt me. India wouldn't let me. I had to stand still and, worse, ask for help. My policy of containment and disappearance didn't stand up at all. The moment I yielded and accepted help, the locks began to work. Hold it right there, the locks said. Stop running. Stand still.

There is a difference between running away and going on a pilgrimage.

Running away indicates a strong desire to get away from whatever is hurting or causing pain or trouble. Counsellors call it 'doing a geographical': the act of moving across the landscape, trying to lose the source of distress. A curious cruelty is embedded in the action: there is an easy willingness in the runner of ignoring the possibility of causing pain for those left behind. There is recklessness in intense emotion that engenders outrageous behaviour.

Running away in a state of brokenness seems like a natural response. It hurts! I'm leaving! The cost is high: separation from loved ones, loss of country, and distance from the very thing that can heal. Somewhere down the line—and it can be a long time—the soul begins to turn back toward the source of pain and the slow, introspective work of facing up to darkness, of working toward healing and eventual recovery.

A pilgrimage, on the other hand, is entered into with willingness and intention. It can be fraught with doubt and fear, yet the pilgrim keeps going, seeking out sacred places, looking for redemption, insight, deliverance. A pilgrimage is a journey both toward and away. It offers the time and space to sift through the past and contemplate the future. It is about being imbued with the present. A pilgrimage opens the heart, shines a light on the dark crevasses and shadows of the spirit. It is about surrender.

Both actions carry within them the desire to find home, a place of ultimate acceptance.

When, as a young woman, I ran away from the tragedy of my mother's death, I stayed on the run for years, ending up an accidental exile, restless and always searching for a home. This time my journey had been deliberate. I carried with me loss and grief: my twin, my father, my dog, my youth and my dreams. This time I knew, with a conscious and painful willingness, that I was going to face up to it all. There had been too much time spent on the run. My decision was clear now. I wanted freedom. I wanted to sit in my psyche without looking back, without checking if I was right or wrong. I wanted the surety that comes from heartfelt self-acceptance and to reclaim a wonder and delight with life. The pilgrimage would lead me, I hoped, to find home within.

Homer's epic poem *The Odyssey* is about the journey Odysseus takes after the Trojan War. He has to face many obstacles and difficulties. He loses his ships, his men and his riches on his way to Ithaca, his homeland. He succeeds, navigating past seductive sirens, the one-eyed Cyclops and lotus eaters. He keeps travelling and he gets home. All is good, his wife has been faithful, his home is golden ... but then he has to leave Ithaca one more time! The journey home is not neat.

This is the journey of age. We travel, we face difficulties, we succeed, we rest and think all is well, and then we have to get up and press on again. We have no choice.

Egyptian poet Cavafy writes about the voyage we all take:

Keep Ithaka always in your mind.
Arriving there is what you are destined for.
But don't hurry the journey at all.
Better if it lasts for years,
so you're old by the time you reach the island,
wealthy with all you've gained on the way,
not expecting Ithaka to make you rich.

CP Cavafy, *Ithaka*

This, then, was the path. I had to meet loss and grief. I had to learn the painful lessons and I had to keep going. I could do it in exotic places, but always, always, I would have to go home.

On my pilgrimage I needed to learn about riches and love and all the attendant losses, and that I should not expect to be understood in either my private quest or my state of grief. And what did I learn? I learned to be still, to listen. Follow the thin red thread. Go to the quiet places. Stand in the Thin Space. Be with animals. Observe rituals. Visit wise people. Go home. Do washing.

The affliction of grief is a sacred place, where ways of knowing and acting are all upside down and there are opportunities you may not normally be able to see. Although your heart may have been torn open, there is love everywhere when you are awake in all your senses.

CHAPTER THIRTEEN

Jigsaw redemption

Everyone gets to walk the dark path and it can be at any stage of life. Grief is not only the preserve of the dignified state funeral or the organised occasion when a well-mannered family mourns the passing of a beloved elder. Secret, hidden and difficult sadnesses visit us all at any time. We are never ready.

Old or young, everyone has access-all-areas passes to the land of pain. Sometimes we're better at getting through than others. We emerge wounded and eventually recover. The stories of those woundings shape the way we move through life from that moment on.

I thought about eighteen-year-old Seth. When his older brother died, fighting in a distant war, Seth became moody and withdrawn. The unresolved nature of the combat and the conflicting politics around it meant his brother's death was not as a clear hero, but rather a casualty in an obscure political game. Seth stayed in his apartment, sunk in gloom, paralysed, with no place to put his anger and sorrow.

One day his cousin brought over a jigsaw puzzle. 'If you won't come out with me,' she said, 'then do this.' After she left, Seth glared at the box with its bright cover picture of a pastoral scene, a river edged with willow trees.

For several days the box sat, gleaming at him, until, with a grunt, he took it down from the shelf, cleared the table and began. Do the edge first, he said to himself as he propped the picture up against a jug, and the rest will follow.

The puzzle was large and complicated, the colours of the trees blending into each other, the river a slick shaft of murky green and blue. Each day Seth would make coffee, light a cigarette, sit down at the table and begin. Some days progress was very slow, then others would offer a breakthrough and a tree would emerge. Soon the side of a building began to appear. Seth looked at the box. There were no structures in the picture. He pressed on. A small cottage sat next to the stream. Then a man with a dog at his side, sitting by an outdoor fire. Slowly and carefully Seth completed the puzzle. When his cousin came over, she laughed.

'Some trickster swapped the covers,' Seth said, 'but they couldn't fool me. I finished it.'

The cousin looked at him. She noticed a slight lifting of the grey dullness in his eyes. His coffee cup was on the bench, washed, his ashtray emptied. It wasn't much, but it was the beginning of Seth walking out of the murky swamp of grief.

And yet.

A few years ago, in a coastal town near where I live, five youths piled into a car and began the drive home from a party. It was a wet night. The car slid off the road during an overtaking manoeuvre. Four of the boys died, but the driver survived unscathed. He was convicted of causing their deaths and, at the age of nineteen, was sent to jail.

The accident was shocking for the seaside village. The boys were known to many; the families' grief was communal. The pain and suffering were palpable. Four young men on the brink of life, dreams extinguished, hopes dashed.

I worried about the young man in jail. What heavy burden of grief would he carry for the rest of his life? How would he recover, if at all?

I was no better at understanding grief and loss than ever. My own losses seemed shallow compared to horrors such as these that others faced, but it didn't make them any less painful. I noticed, as time elapsed after the death of my twin, that a couple of things happened. The world, now rearranged, went back to functioning (relatively) normally. My irritability increased, and the wonderful clarity I had had in the crisis time went away. Of course, in the darkling hours when I couldn't sleep, the hag of depression would come knocking at my bedroom door. I would let her in and allow her to call up my sorrows one by one. As the dawn of a new day arrived she would disappear, and I would begin the process of coping all over again.

There are times when we are so desperately consumed with darkness that it seems there will never be any respite. The jigsaw puzzle gave Seth a pathway. He had to start at the edges and construct a new image of himself until the old one was gone. Jigsaw puzzles teach patience, stillness and attention. Patience derives from the Latin word *patior*, meaning to suffer, to endure. And how did that young man in jail survive? What would a custodial sentence give him, I wondered?

I could talk all I liked about the merit of patience and how it offers a hand when you are tripping over the stumbling stones of grief, how it teaches the deep and lasting lesson of endurance. But are there, I wondered, such things as simpler griefs? Are some people just unlucky? Are some more resilient than others?

I went out onto the verandah and watched another lovely sunset. Here we all are, I thought, everyone battling on in one way or another. Inside, we are all messed-up jigsaw puzzles, with a picture of what we thought or hoped we should be, but which won't match with what we actually are. Throw in some serious griefs and lifelong woundings, and the puzzle has missing pieces and wonky edges. Coming to terms with the beauty and strength of your own crazy, mismatching puzzle seems to be life's work.

Grief and loss. Loss and grief. All I knew was that, young or old, we will all have to walk the dark path. We don't get to decide the when or the how of it. We can linger there, get stuck, we can follow the signs, we can get angry, we can wail and we can shout at the world. None of this changes anything. The dark path has a heart; it speaks to our unfathomable souls and deep longings, and it shows us the world in unimagined ways. The thing of it, the heartbreaking, unnerving, unavoidable thing of it is this: we all have to walk it until we reach the end.

A letter

Dear Angus,

I was thinking about coming to see you, my twin, when I heard you had died. Suddenly and alone, you had gone. I thought I would break in two. You didn't wait for me. My heart clenched in pain.

It's impossible to explain what being a twin is like. We had never been alone. Even before we were born, we were together. We survived a brutal and terrifying childhood, where small misdemeanours—like dropping a dish while washing up—invited a beating with a switch cut from a tree in the garden. I knew how much you suffered, yet I was unable to protect you from the wrath of our father. I did my best to save and support you, and shared everything with you (although there were times when I longed for a birthday party that was just about me).

At school I saw you do your best to cope and make a path in a world where every bully would take out their spite on you. Sometimes the pain seemed more than we could bear. Other times we would run and hide, laughing our heads off, safe for the moment. Then I saw you struggle under the blow of our mother's death when we were teenagers.

Now that you are gone, I am bereft. I feel I was unable to spare you pain and to bring you happiness. But it wasn't my responsibility, I was told. (Try telling that to a twin. The relationship is in the bones, a blood-deep knowing.)

It's been a year now, dear brother, and I know I will mourn the loss of you in my life and grieve for you always. I am glad you are no longer suffering. You wore pain so quietly. The damage you sustained from the daily beatings and steady humiliation was too much for anyone to bear, and I watched you sink into loneliness and depression. I could only watch helplessly, and to protect myself from it—as I could feel what you felt—I moved away. Too far away.

I have made a wee shrine for you in my garden, and I greet you every day when I have my morning cup of tea. I must learn the difference between solitude and loneliness. I will take it upon myself to be a better woman and give thanks for knowing you and loving you in my own inadequate way. Every day without you requires a squaring of the shoulders and a fresh resolution to be brave and to be okay. Angus, I will get better at it as I go along without you. It's going to take me some time. Twinless.

All love, always,
Airdre

Acknowledgements

This book is an accumulation of what I found, saw, heard, remembered and read as I travelled the painful path of loss. We all hold a piece of each other's stories. There is a group of people who have contributed to my understanding of grief. This work is the result of the encouragement and guidance of friends, strangers, colleagues and family.

Thanks to Fran Berry from Hardie Grant (no relation), for asking me to write it, and to Rihana Ries, for helping refine the work. Thanks also to Nikki Lusk, for removing the dangling participles and other vexing grammatical conundrums.

Eben Venter and Rosa Shiels were my mentors and both helped me hugely, honing the words and sharpening the focus. Chris Morgan, Lee Dunn and Victor Marsh from my writing group offered encouragement and sage advice. Friends Caroline

Taggart, Judy Arpana and Rosalba Courtney helped steer the boat when it threatened to wobble off course.

I value and appreciate my sister, Leith Wallace, and brother, Malcolm Grant, who both know this dark path. My daughters, Rosie and Hanne Grant, continue to stand firmly by me with their unwavering love and support.

About the Author

Airdre Grant, a New Zealander by birth, lives in northern New South Wales, Australia. There she works as an academic at Southern Cross University, where she completed a PhD on the relationship between spirituality and health. Her life has been instinctual rather than carefully planned, less a tale of remarkable success and more of a muddling through. She can often be found sitting on her verandah above the township of Lismore, contemplating her next move. Since her daughters left home, she finds herself engaged in a subtle, ongoing power struggle with her large ginger cat, Gordon.